Tonight AT THE LOUNGE

PIANO
VOCAL
GUITAR

ISBN 0-7935-9538-X

HAL•LEONARD®
CORPORATION
7777 W. Bluemound Rd. P.O. Box 13819 Milwaukee, WI 53213

Visit Hal Leonard Online at
www.halleonard.com

Tonight AT THE LOUNGE

CONTENTS

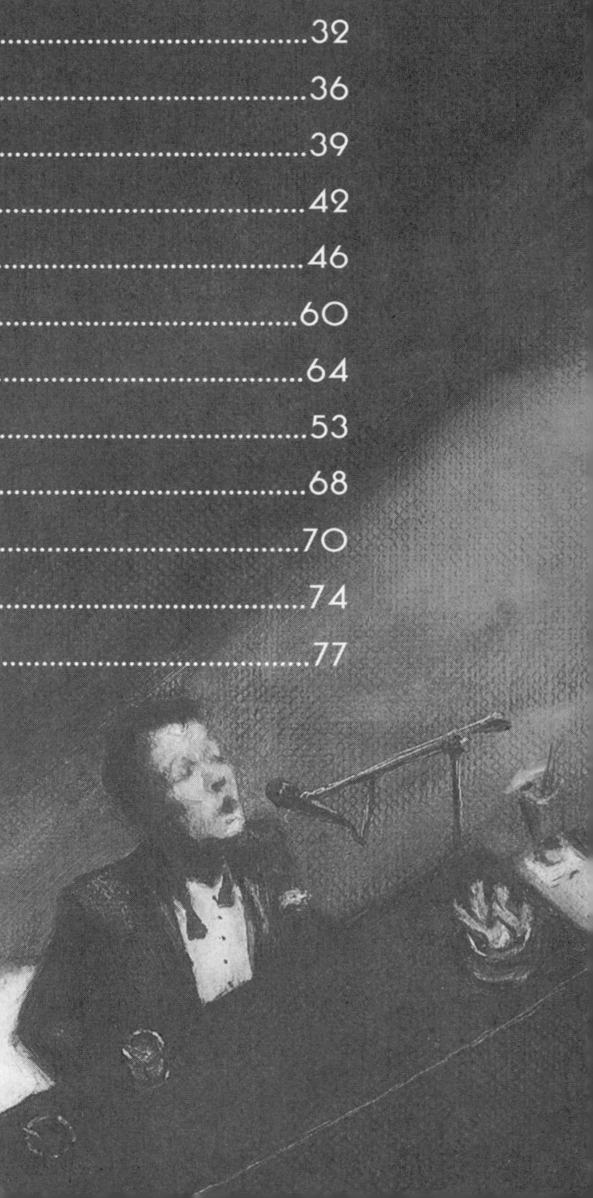

ALL OF ME

Words and Music by SEYMOUR SIMONS
and GERALD MARKS

D7
G7
Take my arms I'll nev - er use them,
C
E7
Your good - bye left me with eyes that cry,
A7
Dm
How can I go on dear with - out you.
Fm
C
Gm
A7
Fm
You took the part that once was my heart, so why not take
G7
1 C
Ab7
Dbmaj7
G7
2 C
Fm
C
All Of Me
Me.

ARE YOU LONESOME TONIGHT?

Words and Music by ROY TURK
and LOU HANDMAN

C
C7
called you sweet - heart
Do the chairs in your
F
Cm
D7
par - lor seem emp - ty and bare
Do you gaze at your
G7
F♯7
G7
C
door - step and pic - ture me there
Is your heart filled with
C7
D7
G7
pain Shall I come back a - gain
Tell me, dear, Are you
1
C
E♭dim
G7
2
C
Lone - some To - night?
Are you
night?

ARRIVEDERCI ROMA
(Goodbye To Rome)
from the Motion Picture SEVEN HILLS OF ROME

Italian Words by PIETRO GARINEI and SANDRO GIOVANNINI
English Words by CARL SIGMAN
Music by RENATO RASCEL

D7 Am7 D7 Am7
mil - lion moon - lit plac - es, cit - y of a mil - lion warm em -
D7 Am7 D7 Cm D7 G Bb7
brac - es. Where I found the one of all the fac - es far from home.
Am7 D7 G Cm D7 G
Ar - ri - ve - der - ci, Ro - ma.
B7 B7+5
It's time for us to

C E7 Am D7 Am7
part. Save the wed-ding bells for my re-
D7 Am7 D7
turn-ing, Keep my lov-er's arms out-stretched and yearn-ing, Please be sure the
Am7 D7 Am7 D7-9 1 G Am7 D7
flame of love keeps burn-ing in her his heart. Ar-
2 G Cm6 G
heart.
rit. e dim.
p

BÉSAME MUCHO
(Kiss Me Much)

Music and Spanish Words by
CONSUELO VELAZQUEZ
English Words by SUNNY SKYLAR

Dm E7♭9 A7 Dm Gm6 Dm
hold me, my dar - ling, and say that you'll al - ways be mine.
que ten - go mie - do per - der - te, per - der - te o - tra vez.
Gm Dm A7 Gm6
This joy is some - thing new, my arms en - fold - ing you, nev - er knew this thrill be -
Quie - ro te - ner - te muy cer - ca, mi - rar - me en tus o - jos, ver - te jun - to a
Dm Gm Dm
fore. Who - ev - er thought I'd be hold - ing you close to me,
mí, pien - sa que tal vez ma - ña - na yo ya es - ta - ré
E7 B♭7 A7 Dm Gm6 Dm
whisp - 'ring "It's you I a - dore;" Dear - est one, if you should
le - jos, muy le - jos de ti. Bé - sa - me, bé - sa - me

Gsus(add2) Gm Gm/B♭ Adim7 Gm A7
leave me, each lit - tle dream would take wing and my life would be
mu - cho, co - mo si fue - ra es - ta no - che la úl - ti - ma
Dm A7/E Dm/F D7 Csus2/E D7/F♯ D7♭9 D+
through. Bé - sa - me
vez; bé - sa - me
Gsus(add2) Gm Dm E7♭9 A7 A7♯5
mu - cho, love me for - ev - er and make all my dreams come
mu - cho, que ten - go mie - do per - der - te, per - der - te des -
1 Dm B♭9 A7sus A7
true.
pués.
2 Dm Gm6 Dm
true.
pués.
R.H.
rit.

THE BIRTH OF THE BLUES

from GEORGE WHITE'S SCANDALS OF 1924

Words by B.G. DeSYLVA and LEW BROWN
Music by RAY HENDERSON

A♭7 G7 A♭7 G7 A♭7 G7
— were search-ing for a diff-'rent tune, one that they could croon as on-ly they
C F C F C A7/E E♭6 G7/D C7
can. — They on-ly had the rhy-thm so —
rit.
a tempo
B7 B♭7
— they start-ed sway-ing to and fro. —
A♭7 G7 A♭7 G7 A♭7 G7
— They did-n't know just what to use, that is how the blues re-al-ly be-

C F C F C A7 A♭7 G7 C G7
gan. They heard the breeze in the trees
rit.
a tempo
G+ C/E E7 F D7
singing weird melodies and they made
G7
that the start of the
C A7 A♭7 G7 C
blues. And from a jail came a wail

G7 G+ C/E E7 F D7
of a down heart - ed frail, and they played
G7
that as part of the
C
no chord
E7 Bm7♭5 E7
blues. From a whip - poor - will out on a hill,
Bm7♭5 E7 Bm7♭5 E7 Bm7♭5 E7 Bm7♭5 E7
no chord
they took a new note, pushed it through a

A7
Am7/D
D7
G7
Am7
A♭7
G7
horn 'til it was worn in - to a blue note! And then they
C
G7
G+
C/E
E7
F
D7
nursed it, re - hearsed it, and gave out the news that the south - land gave birth to the blues!
G7
1 C
A♭7
G7
They heard the blues!
2 C
B♭7
A♭7
C
rall.

BLAME IT ON THE BOSSA NOVA

Words and Music by BARRY MANN
and CYNTHIA WEIL

Moderately
F
I was at a dance
when she caught my eye,
is my bride to be
C7
Stand-in' all a-lone,
look-in' sad and shy.
And we're gon-na raise
a fam-i-ly
F
We be-gan to dance,
sway-in' to and fro
And when our kids ask
how it came a-bout,

Bb
F
C7
And soon I knew I'd nev - er let her go.
I'm gon - na say to them with - out a doubt,
F
C7
Blame it on the Bos - sa No - va with its mag - ic spell,
F
C7
Blame it on the Bos - sa No - va that she did so well.
F
Bb
Oh, it all be - gan with just one lit - tle dance,
But soon it end - ed

F
C7
up a big ro - mance.
Blame it on the Bos - sa No - va,
F
C7
No, no, the
the dance of love.
Now was it the moon
Bos - sa No - va!
F
No, no, the Bos - sa No - va!
C7
Yeh, yeh, the
or the stars a - bove?
Now was it the tune?
the
Bos - sa No - va!
F
Bb
F
1
2
Bos - sa No - va!
the dance of love.
Now that lit - tle girl

CABARET
from the Musical CABARET

Words by FRED EBB
Music by JOHN KANDER

Moderately
mf
Eb
Bb9
Bb9+5
Eb
Bb7+5
What good is sit - ting a - lone in your room?
Put down the knit - ting, the book and the broom,
mp - mf
Eb
Ebmaj7
Eb7
Come hear the mu - sic play;
Time for a hol - i - day;
Ab
Adim
Gm
C9
Fm7
Life is a cab - a - ret, old chum,
Come to the

Bb9
1
Eb
Fm7
Bb9
2
Eb
cab - a - ret.
ret.
Come taste the
Abm
Eb
Cm
Cm+7
wine,
Come hear the band,
Come blow the horn, start
Cm7
F9
Bb7
Eb
cel - e - brat - ing, Right this way, your ta - ble's wait - ing.
No use per -
Start by ad -
Bb9
Bb9+5
Eb
Bb7+5
Eb
Ebmaj7
mit - ting some proph - et of doom
To wipe ev - 'ry smile a -
mit - ting from cra - dle to tomb
is - n't that long a

Bbm7 Eb7 Ab Adim To Coda Gm7 C9
way; stay;
Life is a cab - a - ret, old chum,
Fm7 Bb11 Eb D.S. al Coda
Come to the cab - a - ret,
Come taste the
CODA Gm7 C9 Ab Adim Gm7 C9
ret, old chum,
On - ly a cab - a - ret, old chum,
Fm7 Bb11 Eb Bb9+5 Eb
so come to the cab - a - ret.
sfz
8va

CHICAGO
(That Toddlin' Town)

Words and Music by
FRED FISHER

C D7 E♭7
Bet your bot-tom dol-lar you lose the blues in Chi-ca-go, Chi-
Am7 D7 C♯dim7 Dm7 G9 Dm7 G9 Fdim7
ca-go. The folks who vis-it all wan-na set-tle
Em7 E♭9 Dm7 G7sus C Dm7 Em7 A7
down. On State Street, that great street, I
Dm7 G7 Dm7 G7 A7♯5 Dm7 G7
just wan-na say, (just wan-na say,) they do things they

Bm7 E7 Am A7
don't do on Broad - way. Say,
F B♭9 C/G G7♯5
you'll have the time, the time of your life. Bring all your friends, your kids
C/G E♭dim7 G7 A♭7 G7
and your wife to Chi - ca - go, Chi - ca - go, my home town.
1 C Em7 E♭9 Dm7 G7sus
2 C Em7 E♭m6 Dm7 D♭maj7 Cmaj7
Chi -
2 fr
4 fr

CAN'T SMILE WITHOUT YOU

Words and Music by CHRIS ARNOLD,
DAVID MARTIN and GEOFF MORROW

Moderately, with a relaxed beat

Am
C/D
you on-ly knew what I'm go-ing through; I just can't smile with-out
G
C/D
G(add 9)
G
Em7
you. You came a-long just like a song and
Am7
C/D
D7
G(add 9)
G
Em7
bright-ened my day. Who'd-a be-lieved that you were part of a dream. Now it all seems
Am7
D7
C/E
D7/F#
G
light-years a-way. And now you know I Can't Smile With-out You.
Em
Am
I Can't Smile With-out You. I can't laugh and I can't sing I'm

C/D
Db/Eb
Ab
find-ing it hard to do an - y - thing. You see, I feel sad when you're sad.
cresc.
mf
Fm
Bbm
I feel glad when you're glad. If you only knew what I'm going through;
Db/Eb
Ebm7
I just can't smile. Now, some peo-ple say hap-pi-ness takes
Ab7
Dbmaj7
Dbm
so very long to find. Well, I'm find-ing it hard leav-ing your love be-hind
Eb7sus
E7sus
A
me. And you see, I Can't Smile With - out You.
f

F#m
Bm
I Can't Smile With - out You. I can't laugh and I can't sing. I'm
D/E
Eb/F
Bb
find- ing it hard to do an - y - thing. You see, I feel glad when you.
cresc.
ff
Gm
Cm
you're glad. I feel sad when you're sad. If you on- ly knew what
Instrumental till fade
Eb/F
Repeat and Fade
I'm go-ing through; I just can't smile with- out

CRY ME A RIVER

Words and Music by
ARTHUR HAMILTON

Fm7
Bb7
Fm7
Eb6
Ebdim
Abm6
I cried a riv - er o - ver you.
Cm
Ab
Cm6
Cm7
Fm7
Gm
Bb7#5
Now you say you're sor - ry for be - in' so un -
Ebmaj7
Dm7
G7
Gm7
Gdim
C7#5
true, well, you can cry me a riv - er,
F9
Fm7
Bb7
Fm7
cry me a riv - er, I cried a riv - er o - ver

A la Bach (slightly faster)
Eb6 Cm6 D7b9 Gm
you. You drove me, nearly drove me
Cm6 D7 Gm Gm6
out of my head, while you never shed a tear,
Cm6 D7 Gm
Remember? I remember
Cm6 D7sus D7 G
all that you said; told me love was too plebeian,

Dm7 G7 Cm A♭
told me you were thru with me, an' now you say you
Cm6 Cm7 Fm7 Gm B♭7#5 E♭maj7 Dm7 G7
love me, well, just to prove you do, come on, an'
Gm7 Gdim C7#5 F9
cry me a riv - er, cry me a riv - er,
Fm7 B♭7 Fm7 E♭6 G7#5♭9 E♭6
I cried a riv - er o - ver you. you.
1
2
Ped.

DOWNTOWN

Words and Music by
TONY HATCH

Medium Rock

mf
G
Gmaj7
C
D7
G
When you're a - lone and life is mak - ing you lone - ly, you can al - ways go
Don't hang a - round and let your prob - lems sur - round you, there are mov - ie shows
(Instrumental)
C
D
G
Gmaj7
C
D7
down - town. When you've got wor - ries, all the noise and the hur - ry seems to
down - town. May - be you know some lit - tle plac - es to go to where they

G C D G
help, I know. Down - town. Just list - en to the mu - sic of the
nev - er close. Down - town. Just list - en to the rhy - thm of a
And you may find some - bod - y kind to
f
Em G Em
traf - fic in the ci - ty. Ling - er on the side - walk where the ne - on signs are pret - ty.
gen - tle Bos - sa No - va. You'll be danc - ing with 'em too be - fore the night is ov - er,
help and un - der - stand you. Some - one who is just like you and needs a gen - tle hand to
Bm C
How can you lose? 1,2.The lights are much bright - er there, you can for -
hap - py a - gain.
guide them a - long. 3. So, may - be I'll see you there, we can for -
mf
Em7 A Em7 A G Gmaj7
get all your trou - bles, for - get all your cares. So go down - town,
get all our trou - bles, for - get all our cares. So go down - town,

Am7 D6 D9 G Gmaj7 Am7 D6 D9
things-'ll be great when you're down - town. No fin - er place, for sure,
where all the lights are bright down - town, wait - ing for you to - night
things-'ll be great when you're down - town, Don't wait a min - ute more
G Gmaj7 Am7 D6 D9 1,2 G Am7
down - town. Ev - 'ry-thing's wait - ing for you
down - town. You're gon - na be al - right now
down - town. Ev - 'ry-thing's wait - ing for
Gmaj7 Am7 G Am7 Gmaj7 Am7 3 G Am7
down - town. you
mf
G Am7 G Am7 G Am7 Gmaj7
Down - town. Down - town.

FLY ME TO THE MOON
(In Other Words)
featured in the Motion Picture ONCE AROUND

Words and Music by
BART HOWARD

Bossa Nova

Am7-5 Bb7+5 Gm7 C7
hold my hand! In
Fm7 Ab/Bb Bb7+5 Abdim Eb6 Dm7 G7-9
oth - er words, dar - ling kiss me!
3 3
Cm7 Fm7 Bb7 Ebmaj7
Fill my heart with song, and let me sing for-ev-er more;
Ab Dm7-5 G7-9 Cm C7
You are all I long for all I wor - ship and a - dore. In
4- 4- 3-

Fm7
Ab/Bb
D7-9
1
Gm7-5
C9
Cmaj7
oth - er words,
please be
true!
In
Fm7
Ab/Bb
Bb9
Eb(add9)
oth - er words,
I love you.
2
Gm7-5
C7(#9)
Fm7
Ab/Bb
true!
In
oth - er words,
Bb9
Bb7-9
Eb6
Guitar Tacet
I love you!
8va

GEORGIA ON MY MIND

Words by STUART GORRELL
Music by HOAGY CARMICHAEL

A7
D7
D7♯5
D7
G9
C7
blos-soms fall and all the world's a song,
F
A7♯5
A7/D
Dm
Dm7
G7
D♭dim7
C7(add13)
3 fr
F
I'll go back to Geor - gia 'cause that's where I be - long.
F
A7
Dm
Geor - gia, Geor - gia, the whole day
Gm
3 fr
B♭m
F
E7
Gm
3 fr
G9
C7
F
F♯dim
through. Just an old sweet song keeps Geor-gia on my mind.

Gm7 C7♯5 F A7
3 fr
(Geor - gia on my mind.) Geor - gia, Geor - gia,
Dm Gm B♭m F E7
3 fr
a song of you comes as sweet and clear as
Gm G9 C7(add13) F6 E♭9 F A7 Dm Gm6
3 fr 3 fr 3 fr
moon - light through the pines. Oth - er arms reach
Dm B♭7 Dm Gm6 Dm7 G7
3 fr
out to me, oth - er eyes smile ten - der - ly,

Dm Gm6 3 fr Dm7 E7 Am F♯dim Fm6
still in peace - ful dreams I see the road leads back to
Am C7 F A7 Dm
you. Geor - gia, Geor - gia, no peace I
Gm 3 fr B♭m F E7 Gm 3 fr G9 C7(add13) 3 fr
find, just an old sweet song keeps Geor - gia on my
1
F Dm Gm7 3 fr C7(add13) 3 fr C7♯5
mind.
2
F B♭13 5 fr C7♯5 F6
mind.
rit.

I WILL SURVIVE

Words and Music by DINO FEKARIS
and FREDDIE PERREN

Cmaj7
Gm7
3 fr
I was pet - ri - fied
I had not to fall a - part
Fmaj7
think - ing I could nev - er live with - out you by
try - ing hard to mend the piec - es of my bro -
B♭9
Cmaj7
my side.
ken heart.
And I spent so man - y nights
And I spent so man - y night
Gm7
3 fr
think - ing how you did me wrong, but I grew
feel - ing sor - ry for my - self. I used to

Fmaj7
B♭9
strong. I learned how to get a - long.
cry, but now I hold my head up high.
G/C
Gm7
3 fr
So, you're back from out - er space.
And you see me, some - bod - y new.
C9
Fmaj7
I just walked in to find you here with that sad look
I'm not that chained - up lit - tle per - son that's still
B♭9
Cmaj7
up - on your face. I should - 've changed all the locks.
in love with you. But so you feel like drop - ping in

Gm7
3 fr
I should-'ve made you leave your key if I'd-'ve
and think-ing that I would be free, but now I'm
Fmaj7
Bm7
2 fr
E7sus
known for just one sec-ond you'd be back to both-er me.
sav-ing all my lov-ing for some-one who's lov-ing me.
Am7
Gm7
3 fr
Oh, now go, walk out the door.
B♭/C
Fmaj7
Bm7
2 fr
E7
Just turn a-round now, 'cause you're not wel-come an-y-more.

E7♭9/G♯
Am7
Gm7
4 fr
3 fr
Weren't you the one who tried to hurt me with good-bye?
B♭/C
Fmaj7
Bm7(add11)
E7
2 fr
Did you think I'd crum - ble?
Did you think I'd lay down and die?
E7♭9
Am7
Gm7
3 fr
Oh, no, not I.
I will sur - vive.
B♭/C
Fmaj7
Bm7(add11)
E7
2 fr
Oh, as long as I know how to love I know I'll stay a - live.

E7♭9/G♯
Am7
Gm7
'Cause I ___ got all my life to live
and I ___ got all my love to give,
B♭/C
Fmaj7
B♭9
and I will sur - vive. ___
I will sur - vive. ___
Yes, sir - ee, yeah, yeah, yeah, _
To Coda
Cmaj7
Gm7
___ yeah.
Fmaj7
B♭9
D.S. al Coda
Weren't you the one who tried to hurt me with good-bye?
Took all ___ the strength _

CODA
Cmaj7
Gm7
3 fr
If you wan-na know, _ do I
vive. Lead vocal ad lib.
Fmaj7
B♭9
need you? No no no no.
No no no no no no no no no no no no
no. I _ will, I _ will,
I _ will, I will sur -
Repeat and Fade

JUST THE WAY YOU ARE

Words and Music by
BILLY JOEL

D/F♯ Bm7 Bm7/E E9 G/A
you're too fa-mil - iar And I don't see you an - y more
D Bm6 Gmaj7 Bm D7
I would not leave you in times of trou - ble
Gmaj7 Gm D/F♯ Am D7 Gmaj7
We nev-er could have come this far mm mm I took the good
Gm6 D/F♯ Bm7 Em7 G/A
times I'll take the bad times I'll take you just the way you are

D Gm G/D D Gm6 G/D D
D Bm6 Gmaj7 Bm D7 Gmaj7
Don't go try-ing Some new fash - ion Don't change the col-
Gm D/F♯ Am7 D7 Gmaj7 Gm
or of your hair mm mm You al - ways have my
D/F♯ Bm7 Bm7/E E9
un - spok - en pas - sion Al - though I might not seem to care

G/A
D
Bm6
Gmaj7
I don't want clev-er con-ver-
Bm
D7
Gmaj7
Gm
D/F♯
Am7
D7
sa-tion I nev-er want to work that hard mm mm
Gmaj7
Gm
D/F♯
Bm7
Em7
I just want some-one that I can talk to I want you just
G/A
D
Gm6/D
G/D
D
Gm6/D
D
D7
the way you are.

G A F♯m7 B7 Em7
I need to know that you will al - ways be
The same old some-
A D Am/C Bb C
one that I knew
Oh What will it take till you be - lieve
Am7 D D7 Gm7 C G/A
in me
The way that I be - lieve in you
D Bm6 Gmaj7 Bm D7
I said I love you and that's for - ev - er
voice tacet on D.S.
instrumental on D.S.

Gmaj7 Gm Gm6 D/F♯ Am7 D7 Gmaj7
And this I prom-ise from the heart mm mm I could not love
Gm6 D/F♯ Bm7 Em7 G/A
you an - y bet - ter I love you just the way you are
D Gm6 G/D D Gm6 G/D D
D.S. al Coda
CODA
D/E E9 G/A D
I don't want

Bm6
G7
Bm
D7
Gmaj7
Gm
clev - er
con - ver - sa - tion
I nev - er
want to work that hard
D/F♯
Am7
D7
Gmaj7
Gm6
D/F
mm
I just want
some - one
that I can talk
Bm7
Em7
G/A
Bb
C
to
I want you
just
the way you are
Am7
D7
Gm7
A7
Dmaj7
Whoa

IT NEVER RAINS
(In Southern California)

Words and Music by ALBERT HAMMOND
and MICHAEL HAZLEWOOD

Moderately
f
Am7
D
G
Got on board a west bound sev - en for - ty sev - en,
mf
Am7
D
G
C
Did - n't think before deciding what to do.
G
Am7
D
G
All that talk of op - por - tu - ni - ties T. V. breaks and mov-

Am7
D
G
C6
G
-ies rang true,
sure rang true.
Am7
D
G
Seems It Nev-er Rains In South-ern Cal-i-for-nia,
Seems I've of-
Am7
D
G
Am7
-ten heard that kind of talk be-fore.
It nev-er rains in Cal-i-for-
D
G
Em
Am7
D
-nia, But girl, don't they warn ya, it pours
man, it pours.

G C6 G Am7 D
Out of work, I'm out a' my head,— Out of self re -
G Am7 D G
spect, I'm out— a' bread.— I'm un - der - loved, I'm un - der - fed.—— I wan - na go home.
Am7 D G
It nev - er rains in Cal - i - for - nia,—— But girl, don't they warn
Em Am7 D G C6 G
—— ya,— It pours, man,— it pours. Will you

Am7 D G
tell the folks back home I near-ly made it, Had of-
Am7 D G C G
-fers but don't know which one to take. Please don't
Am7 D G Em
tell them how you found me, Don't tell them how you found me Give me a
3
Am7 D G C6 G
D.S. and Fade
break, Give me a break. Seems it

IT'S IMPOSSIBLE
(Somos Novios)

English Lyric by SID WAYNE
Spanish Words and Music by
ARMANDO MANZANERO

Dm7
G7
Bm7♭5
ba - by not to cry, it's just im - pos - si - ble.
na - mos lo más gran - de de es - te mun - do.
E7
Am7
Cm
Can I hold you clos - er to me, and not
Nos a - ma - mos nos be - sa - mos co - mo
G
E7♭9
Am
feel you go - ing through me? Split the sec - ond that I
no - vios nos de - sea - mos y has - ta a ve - ces sin mo -
A7
D7
nev - er think of you? Oh, how im - pos - si - ble.
ti - vo sin ra - zón nos e - no - ja - mos.

Am7 D7 G G6 Gmaj7 G6
Can the o - cean keep from rush-ing to the shore? It's just im -
So - mos no - vios man - te - ne - mos un ca - ri - ño lim - pio y
F#m7♭5 B7 Em
pos - si - ble. If I had you, could I
pu - ro. Co - mo to - dos pro - cu -
Dm7 G7 Bm7♭5 E7
ev - er want for more? It's just im - pos - si - ble. And to -
ra - mos el mo - men - to más os - cu - ro pa - ra ha -
Am7 Cm
mor - row, should you ask me for the world, some - how I'd
blar - nos pa - ra dar - nos el más dul - ce de los

G
E7♭9
get it. I would sell my ver - y soul and not re -
be - sos re - cor - dar de que co - lor son los ce -
Am
D7
1 G
gret it, for to live with-out your love is just im - pos - si - ble.
re - zos Sin ha - cer más co - men - ta - rios so - mos no - vios.
C♯m7♭5
D7
no chord
2 G
Em7
It's im - pos - si - ble. Im - pos - si - ble.
So - mos no - vios so - mos no - vios
Am7
D7
G
Cm6
G
Mm, im - pos - si - ble.
siem - pre no - vios.
rall.

KING OF THE ROAD

Words and Music by
ROGER MILLER

Moderately, with a bounce

p
mp
C F G C
Trail-er for sale or rent, rooms to let fif-ty cents.
Third box-car mid - night train, des - ti-na-tion: Ban-gor, Maine.
F G Guitar Tacet Dm
No phone, no pool, no pets; I ain't got no cig-a - rettes. Ah, but
Old worn - out suit and shoes; I don't pay no un-ion dues. I smoke
C F G C
two hours of push-ing broom buys a eight by twelve four bit room. I'm a
old sto - gies I have found, short but not too big a - round. I'm a

F
G
To Coda
Guitar Tacet
1
man of means by no means, king of the road.
2
G
C
F
G7
I know ev-er-y en-gi-neer on ev-er-y train, all of the chil-dren and
C
F
all of their names, and ev-er-y hand-out in ev-er-y town, and
G
Guitar Tacet
G7
D.S. al Coda (verse 1)
ev'-ry lock that ain't locked when no one's a-round. I sing
CODA
C

THE LADY IS A TRAMP

from BABES IN ARMS

Words by LORENZ HART
Music by RICHARD RODGERS

C9 F Fm6
both - er with peo - ple I hate,
C C+ F6 G9 C G7
That's why the la - dy is a tramp.
mf
C Cm7 Dm7 G7
I don't like crap - games with Bar - ons and Earls,
C Cm7 Dm7 G7
Won't go to Har - lem in er - mine and pearls.

C Cmaj7 C9 F Fm6
Won't dish the dirt with the rest of the girls,
C C+ F G7 C
Guitar Tacet
That's why the la - dy is a tramp. I like the
Fmaj7 G7 Em7 Am
free fresh wind in my hair,
mf
Dm7 G7 C A7 D7 G7
Life with - out care. I'm broke, it's oke,

C Cm7 Dm E7
Hate Cal - i - for - nia, It's cold and it's damp,
Am C+ Am7 1 D7 G7 C Am Dm7 G7
That's why the la - dy is a tramp.
2 D7 D7-5 G7 C Em
la - dy is a tramp.
Cm7 Dm Fm G7 C

THE LAST WALTZ

Words and Music by LES REED
and BARRY MASON

Em7
A7
D
A7 Em7 A7
A lit - tle girl a - lone and so shy
heart was broke in two when you said "good - bye"
I had the
D Dmaj7 Gmaj7 G6 A7 Em7 A7
last waltz with you
Two lone - ly peo - ple to -
D D7+ G
geth - er
I fell in love with you
The
Em7(A Bass) A7
to Coda
1
D
last waltz should last for - ev - er.
to Coda

2
D G Gm
ev - er. It's all o - ver now no-thing left to say Just my
D Ddim Em9 A7 Gmaj7
tears and the orch-es-tra play - ing La la la la la la la la
D. S. al Coda
F#m7 Em Em7 A7 D A7 Em7 A7
la La la la la la la la la la I had the
D. S. al Coda
CODA
D Gmaj7 Dmaj9
ev - er La la la la la la la la la
rall.
molto rit.

LAZY RIVER

Words and Music by HOAGY CARMICHAEL
and SIDNEY ARODIN

D7 D♭7 C7 F♯dim
Up a la - zy riv - er by the old mill - run, that
G7 G6 A♭9 G9
la - zy, la - zy riv - er in the noon - day sun,
C7 C6 D♭7 C7
lin - ger in the shade of a kind old tree;
F C7/G A♭dim F F7 E7 E♭7
Throw a - way your trou - bles, dream a dream with me.

D7
Db7 C7 F#dim
4 fr
Up a la - zy riv - er where the rob - in's song a -
G7
G6 Ab9 G9
4 fr
Bb
Bdim
wakes a bright new morn - ing, we can loaf a - long.
Blue skies up a-bove,
F/C E7 Eb6 D7
G9 C7
F E7 D7
ev - 'ry one's in love,
up a la - zy riv - er,
how hap - py you can be,
G9 C7
1
F
F7 E7 Eb7
2
F Eb6 E6 F6
up a la - zy riv - er with me.
me.

LOVE WILL KEEP US TOGETHER

Words and Music by NEIL SEDAKA
and HOWARD GREENFIELD

Bb
Bb+
Bb6
stop, 'cause I real - ly love ya; stop, I'll be
Bb7
Eb
Bb
F11
To Coda
think - in' of ya. Look in my heart and let love keep us to -
Bb
geth - er.
Bb
geth - er, what - ev - er

Db
Ab
Eb
Young and beau - ti - ful, but
Gb
Bb
Db
Ab
Eb
some-day your looks will be gone. When the oth - ers turn you off,
Gb
F11
D.S. al Coda
who'll be turn - ing you on? I will, I will, I will. I
CODA
Bb
geth - er, what-ev - er.

MAKE IT WITH YOU

Words and Music by
DAVID GATES

Amaj7
G♯m7
I may be climb - ing on rain - bows.
But you be - lieve the things that I do,
F♯m7
but ba - by, here goes.
and we'll see it through.
F♯m7/B
𝄋
Emaj7
Dreams,
Life
dreams,
F♯m7/E
they're for those who sleep.
can be short or long.
they're for those who sleep.

Emaj7
F#m7/B
Life, it's for us to keep.
Love can be right or wrong.
Life, it's for us to keep.
Amaj7
And if you're won - d'ring what this
And if I chose the one I'd
And if I chose the one I'd
G#m7
C#
all is lead - ing to,
like to help me through,
like to help me through,

F♯m7/B
I want to make it with you.
I'd like to make it with you.
I'd like to make it with you.
Emaj7
F♯m7/B
I really think
that we could make it, girl.
Emaj7
1
To Coda

Amaj7
G#m7
F#m7
F#m7/B
2
F#m7/B
Emaj7
F#m7/B
Ba - by, you know
D.S. al Coda
that
CODA
F#m7/B
Emaj7
Repeat and Fade

MANDY

Words and Music by SCOTT ENGLISH
and RICHARD KERR

Moderately
Bb
I re-mem-ber all my life rain-ing down as cold as ice.
Morn-ing's just an-oth-er day; hap-py peo-ple pass my way.
Stand-ing on the edge of time; I've walked a-way when love was mine.
mf
Cm
Shad-ows of a man, a face through a win-dow,
Look-ing in their eyes, I
Caught up in a world of
Yes-ter-day's a dream, I
1 Eb/Bb
Ab
cry-in' in the night, the night goes in-to
F7
2,3,4
Cm/Bb
see a mem-'ry I
up-hill climb-ing, the
face the morn-ing.

Ab F7 Bb Gm Eb
nev - er re - a - lized how hap - py you made me.
tears are in my mind and noth - in' is rhym - ing.
cry - ing on a breeze the pain is call - ing.
Oh, Man - dy well, you came and you gave with - out tak -
F F7 Bb Gm Eb
- ing. But I sent you a - way. Oh, Man - dy well, you kissed me and stopped me from shak -
F F7 To Coda 1 Bb Gm Eb
- ing, and I need you to - day. Oh, Man - dy!
F7 2 Gm Dm Eb
I'm Man - dy

Cm7
F7
D.S. al Coda
CODA
C
Man - dy well, you came
Am
F
G
G7
and you gave with - out tak - ing, but I sent you a - way. Oh Man -
C
Am
F
G
G7
- dy, well you kissed me and stopped me from shak - ing, and I need
C
Am
F
G
F/G
Repeat and Fade
you.

A NIGHTINGALE SANG IN BERKELEY SQUARE

Lyric by ERIC MASCHWITZ
Music by MANNING SHERWIN

*Pronounced "Bar-kley"

Fm7 B♭7 E♭ Cm Gm E♭7
I may be right, I may be wrong, but I'm
This heart of mine beat loud and fast like a
A♭ G7 Cm A♭m6/C♭ E♭ B♭7
per - fect - ly will - ing to swear that when you turned and
mer - ry - go - round in a fair, for we were danc - ing
E♭7 A♭m6 E♭/B♭ Cm Fm7 B♭7 E♭
smiled at me a night-in-gale sang in Ber - k'ley Square.
cheek to cheek and a night-in-gale sang in Ber - k'ley Square.
Am7♭5 D7 G Em7
The moon that lin - gered o - ver
When dawn came steal - ing up all

Am7 D7 Bm7 B♭dim7 Am7 D7
Lon-don town, poor puz-zled moon, he wore a frown.
gold and blue To in-ter-rupt our ren-dez-vous,
G Em7 Am7 D7
How could he know we two were so in love? The
I still re-mem-ber how you smiled and said, "Was
Bm7 Edim Fm7 B♭7 E♭ Cm
whole darn world seemed up-side down. The streets of town were
that a dream or was it true?" Our home-ward step was
Gm E♭7 A♭ G7 Cm A♭m6/C♭
paved with stars; it was such a ro-man-tic af-fair. And
just as light as the tap-danc-ing feet of As-taire. And

E♭ B♭7 E♭7 Fm7♭5 E♭/B♭ Cm
3fr 3fr 6fr 3fr
as we kissed and said "good - night," a night - in - gale sang in
like an ech - o far a - way, a night - in - gale sang in
Fm7 B♭7 E♭ Cm Fm7 B♭7
1
Ber - k'ley Square. How
Ber - k'ley
2
E♭ Cm Fm7 B♭7 B♭m6/D♭ C7
Square. I know 'cause I was there
Fm7♭5 A♭/B♭ B♭7 E♭ Cm A♭m6 E♭
4fr
That night in Ber - k'ley Square.
rall.
3

MY FUNNY VALENTINE

from BABES IN ARMS

Words by LORENZ HART
Music by RICHARD RODGERS

Slowly
Cm Cm+7 Cm7 Cm6
My fun- ny Val- en- tine, Sweet com- ic Val- en- tine,
Ab Fm7 Fm6 G7 Fm G7
You make me smile with my heart.
Cm G7 Cm7 Cm6
Your looks are laugh- a- ble, Un- pho- to- graph- a- ble,
Ab Fm7 Abm Bb7
Yet, you're my fav- 'rite work of art. Is your

Eb Bb7sus Bb7 Eb Bb7sus Bb7 Eb Bb7sus Bb7 Eb Bb7sus Bb7
fig- ure less than Greek; Is your mouth a lit- tle weak, when you
mf
Ebmaj7 G7+5 G7 Cm Abmaj7 Ab6 Ab7 G7
o- pen it to speak are you smart? But
Cm Cm+7 Cm7 Cm6
don't change a hair for me, Not if you care for me,
cresc. poco a poco
Ab D7-5 G7 Cm Eb7
Stay, lit- tle Val- en- tine, stay!
f molto espress.
Ab Abmaj7 Fm7 Bb7 Eb
Each day is Val- en- tine's day.
mf
mf
p

ON A CLEAR DAY
(You Can See Forever)
from ON A CLEAR DAY YOU CAN SEE FOREVER

Lyrics by ALAN JAY LERNER
Music by BURTON LANE

Dm7/G G7 Dm7 G7
star. You feel part of ev- 'ry moun- tain, sea and shore. You can
mf più espr.
Cmaj7 Dm6 A7 D7 Edim Gmaj7
hear, from far and near, a world you've nev- er heard be- fore. And on a clear day,
G Bm7 E9 Bm E9 Am7 G6 Am7 G6 1. Am7 D7
On that clear day You can see for- ev- er and ev- er-
cresc.
G Em Am7 D7 2. Am7 G6 Am7 G6 Am7
more! On a ev- er and ev- er and ev-
mp
p poco rit.
D7 G Em9 Am9 D7 Gmaj7 G
er- more!
mf
accel.
p

ONCE IN A LIFETIME

from the Musical Production STOP THE WORLD - I WANT TO GET OFF

Words and Music by LESLIE BRICUSSE
and ANTHONY NEWLEY

Fm7 Ebmaj7 Eb7 Abmaj7 Gm7-5 C7-9
My once in a life - time, When
Fm7 Gm7 Fm7 Gm Cm7 F7sus F7
I can ex - plore a new and ex - cit - ing land.
Fm7 Bb7 E7-5 Eb
For once in my life - time I
Bbm7/Eb Eb
feel like a gi - ant, I soar like an ea - gle

Ab Bbm Eb7 Bbm7 Eb7 Abmaj7 Gm7
As tho' I had wings, For this is my mo - ment
Fm7 Ebmaj7 Eb7 Abmaj7 Gm7-5 C7-9
My des - ti - ny calls me, And
Fm7 Gm7 Fm7 Dm7/G G7 Cm7 F7-5 Fm7/Bb Bb7
tho' it may be just once in my life - time I'm going to do great
1 Eb Fm7 Bb7
things. Just
2 Eb Bbm7/Eb Eb6/9
things.
f
mf
mp rit.

PHYSICAL

Words and Music by STEPHEN A. KIPNER
and TERRY SHADDICK

Moderately
Am7 Cmaj7 D C/E Am7 Cmaj7
mf
D C/E Am7 Cmaj7 D B/D# Em D/E
Em D/E Am7 Cmaj7
I'm say - in' all the things that I
I've been pa - tient,
D C/E Am7 Cmaj7
know you'll like, mak - in' good con - ver - sa -
I've been good, try'n to keep my hands on the ta -

D
C/E
Am7
Cmaj7
- tion, I got - ta han - dle
- ble, It's get - tin' hard this
G/D
B/D♯
Em
you just right, you know what I mean.
hold - in' back, you know what I mean.
D/E
Am7
Cmaj7
I took you to an in - ti - mate
I'm sure you'll un - der - stand my
D
C/E
Am7
Cmaj7
res - tau - rant, then to a sug - gest - ive mov -
point of view, we know each oth - er men - tal - ly,

D C/E Am7 Cmaj7 G/D
-ie, There's noth-ing left to talk
You've got-ta know that you're
B/D# Em E7
a-bout 'less it's hor-i-zon-tal-ly.
bring-in' out the an-i-mal in me.
C
Let's get phys-i-cal, phys-i-cal,
3rd time
I wan-na get phys-i-cal, Let's

Em
get into physical. Let me hear your body talk,
your body talk, Let me hear your body talk.
3rd time
1, 2. Let's get
3. Let's get
C
physical, physical, I wanna get physical, Let's
animal, animal, I wanna get animal, Let's
Em
get into physical.
get into animal.
Let me hear you body talk, your body talk,

To Coda
1
2
D.S. al Coda
Let me hear your bod - y talk.
Oh, let's get
CODA
C
instrumental
Em
Let me hear your bod - y talk,
Repeat and Fade
Let me hear your bod - y talk,

ONE FOR MY BABY
(And One More For The Road)
from the Motion Picture THE SKY'S THE LIMIT

Lyric by JOHNNY MERCER
Music by HAROLD ARLEN

G7+5 Cm7 Fm7 Gm Abmaj7 Bb11 Eb6 D7 D7+5
One For My Ba - by and one more for the road. I
R.H.
G D G D G7
got the rou - tine, so drop an - oth - er nick - el in the ma - chine, I'm
mp
pp
G D G Dm7 G7
feel - in' so bad, I wish you'd make the mu - sic dream - y and sad, Could
C G C G
tell you a lot, But you've got to be true to your code, Make it

B7+5 Em7 Am7 Gmaj7 Cmaj7 D11 G F#7 G9
One For My Ba - by and one more for the road. You'd
Gm7 C7 Gm7/C Cm7-5 C9 B7+5 E9 A9 D11 G Am7 Bb6 Am7
nev - er know it, But Bud-dy, I'm a kind of po - et and I've got-ta lot - ta things to say, And
Gm7 C7 Gm7/C Cm7-5 C9 Gm7 Eb9 D7+5
when I'm gloom-y, You sim - ply got-ta lis-ten to me, Un - til it's talked a - way, Well,
G D G D G7
that's how it goes And Joe, I know you're get - ting anx - ious to close, So,
mf
pp
3

G D G G Dm7 G7
thanks for the cheer, I hope you did-n't mind my bend-ing your ear, This
C G C G
torch that I've found, Must be drowned or it soon might ex-plode, Make it
B7+5 Em7 Am7 Gmaj7 Cmaj7 D11 B7+5 B7 E7-9 A7 D11 D7-9 G
One For My Ba-by and one more for the road, That long, long road.
R.H.
F9 Bb11 Bb7+5 G Am7 G G6
It's road.
R.H.
mp
p
pp
ppp

PEOPLE
from FUNNY GIRL

Words by BOB MERRILL
Music by JULE STYNE

needing other children
And yet,
Bbm
C7
Fmaj7
F6
G
Bbm6
Gdim
letting our grown up pride
Hide all the need in-
mf
F
Fdim
Gm7
C7
side, Acting more like children, than
E
F7
Gm7
F9
Bb
children.
Lovers
rit.
mp a tempo

F7
Bb
Cm7
F7
are very special people,
They're the
Eb
Bbmaj7
Fm7
3
luck-i-est people in the world.
3
Bb9
Eb
Ebm
With one person,
One very special
Bb
Fm7
Eb
person,
A feeling deep in your soul

F7
B♭
Gm6
B♭6
Gm7
Says: you were half, now you're whole.
No more hun-ger and thirst, But
Cm7
F7
B♭
B♭7
first, be a per-son who needs peo-ple.
Peo-ple who need
mf molto espressivo
E♭
E♭m
E♭
B♭
Cm7
peo-ple
Are the luck-i-est peo-ple in the
f
1
B♭
Gm7
Cm7
F7
2
B♭
Gm7
B♭6
world.
world.
rit.
p

RIVER, STAY 'WAY FROM MY DOOR

Lyric by MORT DIXON
Music by HARRY WOODS

F F#dim C D7 Ab7 G7
you don't need my cab - in, Riv - er, stay 'way from my
C F#m7-5 B7 Em
door. Don't come up any - y
B7+5 B7 Em7 A7
high - er, I'm so all a - lone.
Em G G#dim D7 D7-5 G7
Leave my bed and my fire, that's all I own.

C Dm7 C C7 F F#dim C Em7-5 A7
I ain't break - in' your heart, don't start break - in' my heart,
D7 Ab7 G7 1 C Ab9 G7 Gdim G7
Riv - er, stay 'way from my door.
2 C Ab9 C E7 Am F7
door.
Lord, ain't I been
Oh Lord, you make the
very steady
Am F7 Am F7
faith - ful? And ain't I worked, ain't I tolled in the sweat - in' sun? Oh
riv - er, But won't you try to re - mem - ber that you made me? Oh

Am
1 Bm7 E7-5 A E7
Lord, ain't I come to you and thanked you for all you've done. Oh,
Lord, hear me pray to you,
2 D9 G7 C Dm7
make the riv - er hear my plea: I ain't break - in'
C/E C7 F F♯dim C Em7-5 A7
your heart, don't start break - in' my heart,
D9 A♭7 G7 C/G A♭7 C9
Riv - er, stay 'way from my door.
rall.

ROUTE 66

By BOBBY TROUP

F F13 E♭13 C13 F6 B♭9
It winds from Chi - ca - go to L. A.,
mf
F6 B♭9
more than two thou-sand miles all the way.
f
mf
F6 Gm7 C13
Get your kicks on Route Six - ty Six!
f
F F13 E♭13 C13 F/C B♭9
Now you go thru Saint Loo-ey Jop - lin, Mis-sour-i and
(sing on 2nd)
f

F/C
F7
B♭9
Ok - la - hom - a Cit - y is might - y pret - ty. You'll see Am - ar -
mf
F6/9
F
Bdim
F
Gm7
C7
il - lo, Gal - lup, New Mex - i - co; Flag-staff, Ar - i - zon - a;
3
f
Gm7
C7
F6/C
Cdim7
Gm7/C
C7
don't for - get Wi - no - na, King - man, Bar - stow, San Ber - nar - din - o. Won't
mp
cresc.
f
mf
F6
B♭9
F6
you get hip to this time - ly tip:
f

B♭9
When you make that Cal-i-for-nia trip.
mf
F6 Gm7 C13
Get your kicks on Route Six-ty Six!
f mf
1 F D7 C#7 C7 no chord
If you
mf
2 F B♭6 Bdim7 F/C no chord
Get your
f
Gm7 C13 F E13 F13
kicks on Route Six-ty Six!
dim.
p
f

SLIGHTLY OUT OF TUNE
(Desafinado)

English Lyric by JON HENDRICKS and JESSIE CAVANAUGH
Original Text by NEWTON MENDONCA
Music by ANTONIO CARLOS JOBIM

G7-5
C13
2
Gm
B♭m
F
Seems to me you've changed the tune we used to sing.
Gm6
A
B♭dim
Bm7
Like the bos-sa no-va love should swing.
E7
A
B♭dim
we used to har-mo-nize two souls in
Bm7
E7
A
F♯m7
per-fect time,
Now the song is dif-f'rent and the

Bm7
E7
C
words don't e - ven rhyme, 'Cause you for - got the
C#dim
Dm7
G7
Gm7
mel - o - dy our hearts would al - ways croon And so what good's a heart that's
F#dim
G7
C7
C7-5
F
Slight - ly Out Of Tune. Tune your heart to
G7-5
Gm7
mine the way it used to be, Join with me in

C7
Cm6
D7+5
D7
Gm7
har - mo - ny and sing a song of lov - ing. We're bound to get in
Bbm
Fmaj7
Dm7
G7
tune a - gain be - fore too long. There'll be no De - sa - fi - na - do
Eb9
When your heart be - longs to me com - plete - ly. Then you
G7
Gm7
F6
won't be Slight - ly Out Of Tune, You'll sing a - long with me.

SPANISH EYES

Words by CHARLES SINGLETON and EDDIE SNYDER
MUSIC BY BERT KAEMPFERT

please don't cry.
Span - ish eyes,
This is just a -
please smile for me once
G
dios and not good - bye.
more be - fore I go.
Soon
I'll re - turn,
bring - ing you all the
G7
C
Cm
3 fr
love your heart can hold.
Please

Cm6
G
say Si Si.
Say
D7
G
you and your Span - ish eyes will wait for me.
A♭
4fr
Span - ish eyes,
wait for me, say Si
G
A♭
4fr
G
Si!

STAYIN' ALIVE
from SATURDAY NIGHT FEVER

Words and Music by BARRY GIBB,
MAURICE GIBB and ROBIN GIBB

Bb7
all right. It's O K. And you may look the oth - er way.
all right. It's O K. I'll live to see an - oth - er day.
We can try to un-der - stand the New York Times' ef - fect on man.
Fm7
Wheth-er you're a broth-er or wheth - er you're a moth-er, you're stay - in' a - live, stay-in' a - live.
Feel the cit - y break-in' and ev - 'ry-bod - y shak-in', and we're stay-in' a - live, stay-in' a - live.

Ah, ha, ha, ha, stay-in' a-live, stay-in' a-live. Ah, ha, ha, ha,
Fm
Eb/F
Fm
stay-in' a-live.
Cm7
To Coda
1. Fm7
Well now, I
2. Fm7
Bb7
Life go-in' no-where.

Fm7
Some-bod - y help me.
Some-bod - y help me, yeah.
Bb7
Life go - in' no where.
Some-bod - y help me, yeah.
Fm7
D.S. al Coda (lyric 1)
Stay-in' a - live.
Well, you can tell
CODA
Fm7
Bb7
Life go - in' no - where.

Some - bod - y help me.
Some - bod - y help me, yeah.
Fm7
Bb7
Life go - in' no - where.
Some - bod - y help me, yeah.
Fm7
I'm stay - in' a - live.
Repeat and Fade

SPINNING WHEEL

Words and Music by
DAVID CLAYTON THOMAS

D7
No Chord
Ride a paint - ed po - ny, let the Spin - ning Wheel spin.
L.H.
E7
A7
D7
G
E7
A7
You got no mon - ey, you got no home, Spin - ning Wheel
D7
G
E7
A7
D7
G
all a - lone, Talk - in' 'bout your trou - bles and you, you nev - er learn,
D7
N. C.
Ride a paint - ed po - ny, let the Spin - ning Wheel turn.
L.H.

C
Bb
Ab
4 fr.
Did you find your di - rect - ing sign __ on the straight and nar - row high -
G
C
Bb
- - way, __ Would you mind __ a re - flect - ing sign? __ Just
Ab
4 fr.
G
Ab
4 fr.
let it shine __ with - in your mind, __ and show you __ the
Bb
C
D9
col - ors __ that are real. __

E7
A7
D7
G
Some - one is wait - ing just for you,
Spin-ning Wheel spin-ning true,
Drop all your trou-bles by the
riv - er - side,
N.C.
Catch a paint - ed po - ny on the
Spin - ning Wheel ride.
Fade out
L.H.

THAT OLD BLACK MAGIC

from the Paramount Picture STAR SPANGLED RHYTHM

Words by JOHNNY MERCER
Music by HAROLD ARLEN

i - cy fin - gers up and down my spine. The
Bb9#5/Eb
4 fr
Eb6
Bb9#5
same old witch - craft when your eyes meet mine. The
Eb
3 fr
same old tin - gle that I feel in - side,
cresc. poco a poco
Db
Db7
4 fr
and then that el - e - va - tor starts its ride,
rit.
f a tempo

A♭6
3 fr
A♭m6
4 fr
E♭maj9
and down and down I go, 'round and 'round
dim. poco a poco
C+
Fm7
Emaj7
E♭
3 fr
3
I go like a leaf that's caught in the tide.
p
Cm
3 fr
A♭9♯11
I should stay a - way but what can I do?
mf
G9
C9
I hear your name and I'm a - flame,

Fm
a - flame with such a burn - ing de -
Db9
Abm6
sire that on - ly your kiss
Bb13
can put out the fire. For
pp
p
Eb
you're the lov - er I have wait - ed for,

B♭m7/E♭
6 fr
the mate that fate had me cre-
cresc. poco a poco
E♭9
A♭
4 fr
at - ed for, and ev - 'ry time
f
A♭m6
4 fr
your lips meet mine, dar - ling,
A♭6/9
A♭m6
4 fr
E♭maj7
3 fr
down and down I go, 'round and 'round
dim.
p

C+
Fm7/E♭
I go in a spin, loving the
Fm7♭5/E♭
6fr
B♭7sus/E♭
6fr
spin I'm in, under that old black mag-
rit.
-ic called love!
1
E♭6
That
2
E♭6
love!
a tempo
a tempo
Fm7♭5/E♭
6fr
E♭6/9
rit. e dim.
pp

THAT'S AMORÉ
(That's Love)
from the Paramount Picture THE CADDY

Words by JACK BROOKS
Music by HARRY WARREN

F7/C
3fr
Bdim7
Cm7
3fr
F7
mor - é.
When the
3
world seems to shine like you've had too much wine, that's a -
B♭
mor - é.
Bells will
B♭/D
D♭dim7
ring, ting - a - ling - a - ling, ting - a - ling - a - ling, and you'll sing, "Vee - ta

F7/C
Bdim7
F7/C
F7
bel - la." Hearts will
a tempo
play, tip - py - tip - py - tay, tip - py - tip - py - tay like a gay tar - an -
B♭
(Optional)
tel - la. (Luck - y fel - la.) When the
B♭/D
D♭dim7
stars make you drool just like pas - ta fa - zool, that's a -

F7/C
3fr
Bdim7
Cm7
3fr
F7
mor - é.
When you
dance down the street with a cloud at your feet, you're in
D7/A
A♭7♭5
G7
love.
When you
Cm
3fr
E♭m6
walk in a dream but you know you're not dream - ing, Sig -

B♭
D♭dim7
nor - é,
scuz - za
F7/C
D♭dim7
F7/C
D♭dim7
F7/C
F7
3 fr
me, but you see, back in old Na - po - li, that's a -
1
B♭
E♭6/B♭
4 fr
B♭maj7
Cm7
F7
mor - é.
When the
2
B♭
E♭m6/B♭
B♭
mor - é.

THREE COINS IN THE FOUNTAIN

Words by SAMMY CAHN
Music by JULE STYNE

Eb Fm7 Eb Fm7 Bb7 Fm7 Bb7
bless? Three hearts in the foun - tain,
Fm7 Eb Ebmaj7 Cm7
Each heart long-ing for its home, There they lie in the
F7 Cm7 F7 Abm6 Bb7 Eb Ab
foun - tain Some-where in the heart of Rome. Which one will the foun-tain
Eb Abm Fm7 Bb7-5 Eb
bless? Which one will the foun-tain bless? Three coins in the

Fm7 Bb7 Fm7 Bb7 Fm7 Eb
foun - tain, Through the rip - ples how they shine
Ebmaj7 Cm7 F7 Cm7 F7 Abm6 Bb7
Just one wish will be grant - ed One heart will wear a val - en -
Eb Eb9 Ab Fm7
tine. Make it mine! Make it mine! Make it
1 Eb Ebmaj7 Fm7 Bb9
mine!
2 Eb Ebmaj7 Fm7 Eb
mine!
rall.

UP, UP AND AWAY

Words and Music by
JIMMY WEBB

Moderately
G
F
Would you like to ride in my beau - ti - ful bal - loon?
world's a nic - er place in my beau - ti - ful bal - loon. It
Love is wait - ing there in my beau - ti - ful bal - loon,
mf
Bb
Ab
Would you like to glide in my beau - ti - ful bal - loon? We could float
wears a nic - er face in my beau - ti - ful bal - loon. We can sing
Way up in the air in my beau - ti - ful bal - loon. If you'll hold
Db
Dbmaj7
Db7
Ebm7
Ab9
a - mong the stars to - geth - er, you and I,
a song and sail a - long the sil - er sky,
my hand we'll chase your dream a - cross the sky,
For we can fly!

D♭
E♭m7
D♭
E7
We can fly!
f
A
D
G
Up, up and a - way, my beau - ti - ful, my beau - ti - ful bal -
mf
A
G
F
1
A
G
F
loon! The
f
mf
2
A
G
F
To next strain
3
FINE
A
G
F
Repeat and fade

C
Em
Dm7
G7
Sus - pend - ed un - der a twi - light can - o - py
C
Dm7
G7
We'll search the clouds for a star to guide us.
Eb
Gm
Fm7
Bb7
If by some chance you find your - self lov - ing me, We'll
Gb
Ab
G
F
Eb
D.C. al Fine
find a cloud to hide us, Keep the moon be - side us.

WHO CAN I TURN TO
(When Nobody Needs Me)
from THE ROAR OF THE GREASEPAINT - THE SMELL OF THE CROWD

Slowly with expression

Words and Music by LESLIE BRICUSSE
and ANTHONY NEWLEY

Fmaj7 F Em7 Cmaj7/E Am Am7 Fmaj7 Dm6
and no - one be - side me, I'll go on my way, and
Em7 A7 Dm Dm7 G7
af - ter the day, The dark - ness will hide me; And
Cmaj9 C6 Dm7 G7
may - be to - mor - row I'll find what I'm af - ter
Dm7 G7 C C6 Cmaj7 C
I'll throw off my sor - row, beg steal or bor - row

Gm Gm7 C9 F F+
my share of laugh - ter. With you I could learn to,
Dm6 E7 Am Am(+7) Am7
with you on a new day, But
F C6 Dm7 Db7
who can I turn to if you turn a - way?
cresc.
1 C6 Dm7/C G13
2 C6 Dm7/C G13 Cmaj7 C6
way?
rit. e dim.

WHAT A WONDERFUL WORLD

Words and Music by GEORGE DAVID WEISS
and BOB THIELE

C11 C7 F F+ B♭maj7 C7
What a won - der - ful world. I see
F Am B♭ Am Gm7 F
skies of blue and clouds of white, the bright bles - sed day, the
A7 Dm D♭
dark sac - red night, and I think to my - self
C11 C7 F B♭ F
What a won - der - ful world. The

C7
F
colors of the rainbow, so pretty in the sky are
C7
F
also on the faces of people goin' by, I see
Dm
C/E
Dm/F
C/G
friends shakin' hands, sayin', "How do you do!"
Dm/F
F♯dim
Gm7
F♯dim
C7
They're really sayin' "I love you," I hear

F Am Bb Am Gm7 F
babies cry, I watch them grow They'll learn much more than
simile
A7 Dm Db C11 C7
I'll ever know and I think to my-self What a won-der-ful
F Am7-5 D7 Gm7
Rubato
world. Yes, I think to my-self
C7-9 Slowly F Bb6 F
What a won-der-ful world.
rit.

WHAT KIND OF FOOL AM I?

from the Musical Production STOP THE WORLD - I WANT TO GET OFF

Words and Music by LESLIE BRICUSSE
and ANTHONY NEWLEY

Am7 D7 Gsus G7 Cmaj7
emp- ty heart must dwell. What kind of lips are these
clown am I?
Cmaj7 Dm7(add G) G7 Cmaj7
That lied with ev- 'ry kiss? That whis- pered emp- ty words of
What do I know of life? Why can't I cast a- way the
Gm/B♭ A7 Gm7 C7 F6
love that left me a- lone like this? Why can't I fall in love
mask of play and live my life? Why can't I fall in love
Dm7-5 C/E D7 Dm7
like an- y oth- er man And may- be then I'll know what
'til I don't give a damn
Fm G7 C Cmaj7 Am7 Fmaj7 G7 C Cmaj7 Am7 Fmaj7 Dm7 Cmaj7
kind of fool I am. What kind of am.

WHAT THE WORLD NEEDS NOW IS LOVE

Lyric by HAL DAVID
Music by BURT BACHARACH

D7
Bm7
lit - tle of. What the world needs
Em7
Bm7
Em7
now is love, sweet love,
C6
C
B
To Coda
No, not just for some, but for ev - 'ry - one.
B7
Em7
Lord, we don't need an - oth - er
Lord, we don't need an - oth - er

Dm9
moun - tain, There are moun - tains and
mead - ow, There are corn - fields and
G6/9
Cmaj7
C6
3
hill - sides e - nough to climb; There are
wheat - fields e - nough to grow; There are
Dm7
G7
Cmaj7
o - ceans and riv - ers e - nough to cross, E-
sun - beams and moon - beams e - nough to shine, Oh,
Em7
A7
D9
nough to last, till the end of time.
lis - ten, Lord, if you want to know.

1
Am7/D
2
Am7/D
D.S. al Coda
What the
What the
CODA
B
B7
E7
C6
ev - 'ry - one.
No, not just for some,
3
C
Bm7
Cmaj7
Oh, but just for ev -
D7
G
'ry - one.

A WONDERFUL DAY LIKE TODAY

from THE ROAR OF THE GREASEPAINT - THE SMELL OF THE CROWD

Words and Music by LESLIE BRICUSSE
and ANTHONY NEWLEY

Fm7
1. F7
Bbsus
Bb7
won- der- ful day like to- day. On a
won- der- ful morn-
2. F7
Bb7-9
Eb6
tacet
Ab
Ab+
-ing like this. On a morn- ing like this I could
Fm/Ab
Bb7/Ab
Eb/G
Cm7
Bmaj7
Fm7
kiss ev- 'ry- bod- y I'm so full of love and good-
Ebmaj7
Ab
Ab+
will. Let me say fur- ther- more I'd a-
Fm
Bb7
Gm7
Gb+
-dore ev- 'ry- bod- y to come and dine. The plea- sure's mine, And

F7 Fm7/Bb Eb Ebmaj7
tacet
I will pay the bill. May I take this oc- ca- sion to say
Eb6 Eb Fm7
That the whole hu- man race should go down on its knees,
Bb7 F7 Bb7 Gm7
Show that we're grate- ful for morn- ings like these,
C7 Ab6 G7 Cm7
For the world's in a won- der- ful way,
F9 Fm7 Bb7 Eb
On a won- der- ful day like to- day.

WITCHCRAFT

Lyric by CAROLYN LEIGH
Music by CY COLEMAN

F
G#7
Those fin - gers in my hair_ That sly, come - hith - er stare_
Gm7
C7
F
Bb
that strips my con-science bare It's Witch - craft
And I've got
Bbm
Fm
no de - fense_ for it The heat is too in - tense_ for it What good would
G7+5
Cmaj7
C7
Fmaj9
F
com - mon sense for it do? 'Cause it's Witch - craft!_ Wick - ed
C11
C7
Fmaj9
F6/9
Fmaj9
F6
Bm7-5
Witch - craft_ And_ al - though I_ know_ it's strict-ly ta - boo,

E7
Am
F
Am6
When you a - rouse the need in me, my heart says,
F
Am
Gm
Eb
Gm7
"Yes, in - deed" in me, "Pro - ceed with what you're lead - in' me to!"
C7
F#6
F6
G#7
It's such an an-cient pitch But one I would-n't switch
Gm7
E6
1 F6
'Cause there's no nic - er witch than you!
2 F6
you!

YOU'VE LOST THAT LOVIN' FEELIN'

Words and Music by BARRY MANN, CYNTHIA WEIL and PHIL SPECTOR

C
Dm7
You're try - ing hard not to show it,
It makes me just feel like cry - ing,
Em7
Fmaj7
F/G
G
(Ba - by) but, ba - by, ba - by, I know it.
'cause ba - by, some - thing beau - ti - ful's dy - ing.
3
C
Dm/C
G7
You've lost that lov - in' feel - in', woh oh, that lov -
C
Dm/C
- in' feel - in'. You've lost that lov - in' feel - in'! Now it's

B♭/C
1
C
gone, gone, gone, woh oh oh oh.
2
C
F
G
F
G
Now there's no
C
F
G
F
G
C
F
Ba - by, ba - by, I'd get down on my knees for you.
G
F
G
C
F
G
F
G
If that would make you love me like you used to

C F G/F G C F
do.
We had a love, a
G F G C F
love, a love you don't find ev - 'ry day.
G F G C F G F G
So don't, don't, don't, don't let it slip a -
C F G F G C F
way.
Ba - by,
(Bkgd:) Ba - by,

G F G C F
ba - by, I beg you please,
ba - by, beg you please,
G F G C F
please, I need your love, I need your
please, I need your love,
G F G C F
love, so bring it on back, so bring it on
I need your love, bring it on back,
G C
back. Bring back that
bring it on back.

Dm/C
G7
C
lov - in' feel - in', woh oh, that lov - in' feel - in'.
Dm/C
Bring back that lov - in' feel - in', 'cause it's
B♭/C
gone, gone, gone, and I can't go
C
Repeat and Fade
on, woh oh oh oh.

YOU'RE NOBODY 'TIL SOMEBODY LOVES YOU

Words and Music by RUSS MORGAN,
LARRY STOCK and JAMES CAVANAUGH

Am D7 G6 D7♯5
no - bod - y 'til some - bod - y cares. You
Bm7 B♭dim Am7
2 fr
may be king, you may pos - sess the world and it's gold, but
A6/9 A9♯5 A9 Am7 D7 Am7 D7 D7♯5
gold won't bring you hap - pi - ness when you're grow - ing old. The
G B7 E7♭9 E7 B7/F♯ E7/G♯
world still is the same, you'll nev - er change it, as
3

Am
E7
Am
E7/B
sure as the stars shine a - bove.
Am/C
C
C♯dim7
You're no - bod - y 'til some - bod - y loves
G
E7
Am
E7/B
Am/C
A7
D7
you, so find your - self some - bod - y to
R.H.
1
G
F13sus
F9
E♭7sus
E♭7
D9
4 fr
love. You're
2
G
Cm7
3 fr
G6
love.
L.H.